"We have a beautiful

mother

Her green lap

immense

Her brown embrace

eternal

Her blue body

everything

we know."

—ALICE WALKER,
"WE HAVE A BEAUTIFUL MOTHER"
FROM *HER BLUE BODY EVERYTHING
WE KNOW: EARTHLING POEMS*

ALICE WALKER: AFRICAN-AMERICAN AUTHOR AND ACTIVIST

BY LUCIA RAATMA

Content Reviewer: Dr. Donna Haisty Winchell,
Professor of English, Clemson University

Published in the United States of America by The Child's World®
PO Box 326
Chanhassen, MN 55317-0326
800-599-READ
www.childsworld.com

The Child's World®: Mary Berendes, Publishing Director
Editorial Directions, Inc.: E. Russell Primm and Emily Dolbear, Editors; Katie Marsico and
Elizabeth K. Martin, Editorial Assistants; Dawn Friedman, Photo Researcher; Linda S. Koutris,
Photo Selector; Kerry Reid, Fact Researcher; Susan Hindman, Copy Editor; Halley Gatenby,
Proofreader; Tim Griffin/IndexServ, Indexer; Vicki Fischman, Page Production

The Child's World® and Journey to Freedom® are the sole property
and registered trademarks of The Child's World®

Cover photograph: Alice Walker at home in 2000 / © Noah Berger/AP Wide World Photos

Interior photographs © Noah Berger/AP Wide World Photos: 2; Court Mast/AP/Wide World Photos: 6; Jerry
Telfer/AP/Wide World Photos: 8; Orlin Wagner/AP/Wide World Photos: 26, 35; Laura Sikes/AP/Wide World
Photos: 28; Bob Krist/Corbis: 11; Corbis: 13; Joel Katz/Corbis: 17; Ed Eckstein/Corbis: 19; James L.
Amos/Corbis: 20–21; Bettmann/Corbis: 22, 23; Corbis Sygma: 31; Steve Jennings/Corbis: 36; Hulton
Archive/Getty Images: 32; Carl Mydans/Library of Congress: 9; The MacDowell Colony: 18; Diane
Wilson/N.Y. Nathiri: 25; Sarah Lawrence College Archives: 14; Gary Gladstone/Sarah Lawrence College
Archives: 15, 27; Wellesley College Archives: 24.

Library of Congress Cataloging-in-Publication Data
Raatma, Lucia.
Alice Walker : African-American author and activist / by Lucia Raatma.
p. cm. — (Journey to freedom)
"An editorial directions book"—T.p. verso.
Includes bibliographical references and index.
Contents: A brave voice—The early lessons—Writer and activist—Acclaim and criticism—
Prizes and politics—Timeline.
ISBN 1-56766-512-8 (Library Bound : alk. paper)
1. Walker, Alice, 1944– —Juvenile literature. 2. Authors, American—20th century—Biography—
Juvenile literature. 3. Civil rights workers—United States—Biography—Juvenile literature.
4. Social reformers—United States—Biography—Juvenile literature. 5. African American authors—
Biography—Juvenile literature. [1. Walker, Alice, 1944– 2. Authors, American. 3. Civil rights workers.
4. African Americans—Biography. 5. Women—Biography.] I. Title. II. Series.
PS3573.A425Z86 2003
813'.54—dc21
2003004293

Contents

Alice Walker
Author

A Brave Voice

Alice Walker is a leading voice not only among African-American women writers but also throughout the literary world. She is probably best known for *The Color Purple,* a 1982 novel that won the **Pulitzer Prize** for fiction.

Throughout her career, Walker has bravely created works about the world as she sees it. She has also taken a stand on issues that are important to her. In college, she fought for **civil rights.** As she matured, she took on **sexism** both in the United States and in other countries.

Along the way, many people have criticized Walker's outspoken manner. At first, the harsh words bothered her, but that changed as she got older. Now, she embraces her personal views and is eager to share them with others. Walker—famous as a writer, a poet, a **feminist,** and an **activist**—has much to say.

ALICE WALKER HAS SPENT HER LIFE AS A DEDICATED WRITER AND AN INVOLVED ACTIVIST.

The Early Lessons

On February 9, 1944, Alice Malsenior Walker was born in Eatonton, Georgia. The eighth and youngest child in the family, Alice grew up in a tiny shack in a rural part of the state. Her parents, Minnie Tallulah Grant Walker and Willie Lee Walker, were **sharecroppers** without much money. In spite of her modest background, Alice was proud of her family.

As a child, Alice heard stories about Mary Poole, her father's great-great-great grandmother, a slave who once had to walk from Virginia to Georgia carrying a baby in each arm. She learned about Tallulah, her great-grandmother on her mother's side who was part Cherokee Indian. Walker remembers her father's wonderful sense of humor. She credits her mother's strong faith in helping her explore her own **spirituality.**

ALICE WALKER CAME FROM A LARGE FAMILY WITHOUT MUCH MONEY. HER CHILDHOOD EXPERIENCES GREATLY INFLUENCED HER WRITING.

THIS GENERAL STORE WAS LOCATED NEAR ALICE WALKER'S HOMETOWN OF EATONTON, GEORGIA. THE PHOTOGRAPH WAS TAKEN IN THE LATE 1930S.

As a young girl, Alice knew she was pretty. She was outgoing and enjoyed being around other people. She liked performing at church and giving speeches. All that changed in the summer of 1952. One day, while playing with her brothers, Alice was accidentally shot in the eye with a BB gun. A local doctor treated her, but she developed a large white scar on that eye.

Suddenly, Alice's self-image was different. Schoolmates teased her about her appearance, and she became withdrawn. Uncertain of the outside world, Alice retreated into literature. She read a variety of books, and she began to write poetry. She neglected her schoolwork, and her grades fell. During this lonely time in her life, she also began to watch people and study their relationships.

Several years later, when Alice was 14, her brother Bill decided to help her. He found a doctor in Boston, Massachusetts, who could treat her.

The doctor removed the white scar from her eye. What was left was a blue sliver instead, much less noticeable, but she never regained her vision in that eye. Her physical appearance restored, Alice felt confident about herself again. During those years of loneliness, however, she realized that beauty is more than appearance, and she began to appreciate what she had inside.

High school was a promising time for Alice. She was an excellent student and graduated at the top of her class in 1961. She was named prom queen during her senior year. Alice also won a scholarship to Spelman College in Atlanta, Georgia.

When she left for college, she brought along three important gifts from her mother: a sewing machine so she could be self-sufficient and independent; a suitcase so she could feel free to travel; and a typewriter so she could always tell stories. These gifts helped Alice Walker to become the writer she is today.

ALICE WALKER WON A SCHOLARSHIP TO ATLANTA'S SPELMAN COLLEGE, SHOWN HERE IN THE 1990S.

Spelman College, a traditionally African-American college for women, was an interesting place for Walker. While a student there, she joined the civil rights movement.

The 1960s were a difficult time of violence and great change in U.S. history. Walker remembers, "The first protest I joined [was] . . . in 1962. I was 18. It was very cold, snow and sleet everywhere. Our hands and feet and heads were freezing as we trudged in circles, shouting slogans to keep our minds off our misery and to encourage each other."

At the end of her freshman year, she was invited to attend the Youth World Peace Festival in Helsinki, Finland. In honor of this, she was invited to the home of civil rights leader Dr. Martin Luther King Jr. She was thrilled to meet King, and she enjoyed attending the festival. When it was over, Walker traveled in Europe for the summer. The trip marked the start of her love of travel and exploring other cultures.

The following summer, in August 1963, Walker journeyed to Washington, D.C., and participated in the now-famous March on Washington for Jobs and Freedom. There she had the incredible experience of hearing King's "I Have a Dream" speech. At the tender age of 19, she had witnessed history.

After that summer, Walker did not return to Spelman. Instead, she was offered a scholarship to Sarah Lawrence College in Bronxville, New York.

MARTIN LUTHER KING JR. SPEAKS AT THE 1963 MARCH ON WASHINGTON FOR JOBS AND FREEDOM. ALICE WALKER WAS ONLY 19 WHEN SHE ATTENDED THE HISTORIC EVENT.

oving to New York was a big decision for Walker, but she was eager to study at such a well-regarded school as Sarah Lawrence. While a student there, she became more interested in literature and in her own writing. Two professors, poet Muriel Rukeyser and writer Jane Cooper, encouraged her to write and to strengthen her creative talent.

AT SARAH LAWRENCE COLLEGE, WALKER STUDIED WITH MURIEL RUKEYSER, SHOWN HERE. THE PROFESSOR WAS SUPPORTIVE OF WALKER'S WRITING TALENT.

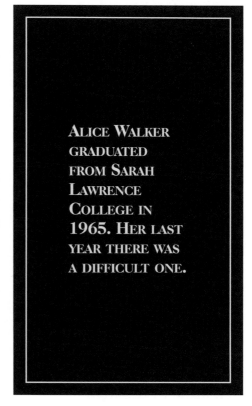

ALICE WALKER
GRADUATED
FROM SARAH
LAWRENCE
COLLEGE IN
1965. HER LAST
YEAR THERE WAS
A DIFFICULT ONE.

During the summer before her senior year in college, Walker took an important trip. She traveled to Uganda as an exchange student. It was an exciting time for her, and she enjoyed learning about African culture. But in her last year at Sarah Lawrence, Walker discovered she was pregnant.

Being young and single and pregnant was scary for Walker, and she worried about what she should do. She was afraid to tell her parents, fearing they would be forever disappointed in her. For a time, she seriously considered ending her life. She wrote pages and pages of poetry, a natural outlet for all of her confused emotions.

Finally, Walker told some of her friends her secret. They talked to her about her options and helped her make a decision. She finally decided to end the pregnancy. Then, Walker fell into a deep **depression.** She withdrew from people, much as she did as a child after the BB gun accident. She focused all her efforts on writing.

While in her depression, Walker thought about her situation. Though she thought about ending her life, she came to understand it was not a solution to her problems. She recalls, "I realized how much I loved [the world], and how hard it would be not to see the sunrise every morning, the snow, the sky, the trees, the rocks, the faces of people."

During this time, she wrote "To Hell with Dying," a short story, as well as a number of poems that were later published in a collection called *Once.* Though her last year of college had been trying for Walker, she managed to use those difficult experiences as a basis of her own creativity. In 1965, Alice Walker graduated from Sarah Lawrence as a wiser young woman, well on her way to being a published writer.

Writer and Activist

After college, Alice Walker returned to her home state of Georgia to work again for civil rights. This time, she helped people register to vote. She then moved to New York City and took a position in the city's **welfare** department. In the meantime, she also earned a writing **fellowship** from the Bread Loaf Writers' Conference in Middlebury, Vermont.

Though her work in New York was challenging, Walker wanted to continue her efforts in the civil rights movement. So in the summer of 1966, she went door to door in Mississippi, helping register people to vote. It was during this summer that she met Mel Leventhal, a young Jewish law student who was also working for civil rights. Walker and Leventhal soon fell in love, and they both returned to New York City, where he attended law school.

LIKE THIS CIVIL RIGHTS WORKER HOLDING A VOTER REGISTRATION POSTER, ALICE WALKER HELPED PEOPLE REGISTER TO VOTE IN MISSISSIPPI IN THE 1960s.

The relationship that Walker and Leventhal shared was one of encouragement and support. While Leventhal pursued his law career, he urged Walker to write.

During this time, Walker wrote "The Civil Rights Movement: What Good Was It?" This essay became her first published article, and *American Scholar* magazine awarded it first prize in its annual essay contest. This success gave Walker confidence, and she hoped to find time to work on a novel. This wish was granted when she won a fellowship at the MacDowell Colony, a well-known artist community in New Hampshire.

ALICE WALKER WORKS IN HER WRITING STUDIO AT THE MACDOWELL COLONY, AN ARTIST COMMUNITY FOUNDED IN NEW HAMPSHIRE IN 1907.

On March 17, 1967, Walker and Leventhal were married and then moved back to Mississippi. There, Leventhal took on civil rights legal cases while Walker continued to work on her novel. Because Leventhal is white and Walker is black, the couple faced threats of violence from many people in the southern state. They did not let such threats stop them.

Leventhal handled cases for the National Association for the Advancement of Colored People (NAACP). Walker taught black history in the local Head Start program, an educational project for young children funded by the U.S. government. During this time, Walker again discovered she was pregnant, and this time, the news was joyful for her.

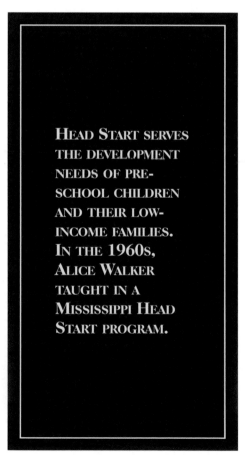

HEAD START SERVES THE DEVELOPMENT NEEDS OF PRE-SCHOOL CHILDREN AND THEIR LOW-INCOME FAMILIES. IN THE 1960s, ALICE WALKER TAUGHT IN A MISSISSIPPI HEAD START PROGRAM.

Walker's joy was short-lived, however. Martin Luther King Jr. was killed on April 4, 1968. Walker understood that his death was a terrible blow to the civil rights movement. She went to his funeral in Atlanta and then returned to Mississippi, but her grief was overwhelming. Perhaps these strong emotions played a part in the next tragedy she experienced: the sudden loss of her unborn baby.

CROWDS FOLLOW MARTIN LUTHER KING JR.'S FUNERAL PROCESSION DOWN AN ATLANTA STREET IN 1968. ALICE WALKER ATTENDED THE FUNERAL.

In spite of these losses, Walker accepted a teaching position at Jackson State University in Mississippi. She continued writing, and the poetry collection that she had begun in college, titled *Once*, was published.

Walker also became pregnant again and finished her first novel, *The Third Life of Grange Copeland*. In fact, she wrote the last lines of the book just days before her daughter, Rebecca Grant, was born.

ALICE WALKER'S DAUGHTER, REBECCA, WAS BORN IN 1969. THE AUTHOR IS SHOWN HERE WITH HER HUSBAND AND DAUGHTER IN 1970.

Acclaim and Criticism

The *Third Life of Grange Copeland* received praise from many literary critics as well as harsh criticism from some African-American readers. The novel tells the story of a woman murdered by her husband. Like Alice Walker's parents, the murderer and his victim were sharecroppers. Many people felt that Walker portrayed black men too negatively. Walker tried not to let such remarks bother her. She stood by her opinion that women are often treated badly by their mates.

The attention Walker got for her first novel earned her recognition from colleges around the country. She accepted the position of writer-in-residence at Tougaloo College in Mississippi. That job was followed by a fellowship from the Radcliffe Institute. Then, in 1972, she was offered a teaching position at Wellesley College in Massachusetts.

ALICE WALKER TALKS ABOUT HER NOVEL *THE THIRD LIFE OF GRANGE COPELAND* IN AN INTERVIEW IN NEW YORK CITY.

At Wellesley, Walker made history by creating a women's literature course, one of the first women's studies courses in the country. As a teacher, she wanted to introduce her students to African-American women writers, something few—if any—college professors were doing. During preparation for the class, Walker discovered the work of Zora Neale Hurston, a writer from the **Harlem Renaissance.**

WALKER, SHOWN HERE IN 1970, TAUGHT AT WELLESLEY COLLEGE. SHE DEVELOPED A LITERATURE COURSE THAT FOCUSED ON WOMAN AUTHORS, INCLUDING ZORA NEALE HURSTON.

Hurston was a gifted author, but at the time of her death in 1960, she was poor and hardly known. Walker was moved by Hurston's writings, including *Mules and Men* and *Their Eyes Were Watching God*. Hurston's life intrigued Walker. She later edited a collection of Hurston's work. Walker appreciated the fact that Hurston's African-Americans were complicated characters with important ideas. Such characters were much different from those often portrayed at that time in books about African-Americans. Walker explains, *"Their Eyes Were Watching God* is riveting immediately, because of the language. You start reading it and you think you won't be able to understand it. And then you realize that you understand it perfectly."

Walker decided she wanted to locate Hurston's unmarked grave. She traveled south to Fort Pierce, Florida, and pretended to be Hurston's niece. Walker was able to learn that Hurston died alone in a nursing home. She also found where Hurston was buried—in a neglected spot covered in weeds. Walker cleared the site and had a headstone placed there.

ZORA NEALE HURSTON'S HEADSTONE, ERECTED BY ALICE WALKER, READS:

"A GENIUS OF THE SOUTH"
1901–1960
NOVELIST   FOLKLORIST
ANTHROPOLOGIST

The following few years were remarkably productive for Walker. In 1973, her father died, and again her emotions fueled her writing. She published *In Love & Trouble: Stories of Black Women*, her first collection of short stories, as well as *Revolutionary Petunias & Other Poems*, a second collection of poetry. She made it a point to write every day, and she became an editor at *Ms.* magazine.

In 1974, she published a young adult book about Langston Hughes. Hughes was an African-American writer who had once written her a note of encouragement, and she had long admired him.

AT A NEWS CONFERENCE IN 2002, ALICE WALKER STANDS NEXT TO A POSTER OF A LANGSTON HUGHES COMMEMORATIVE POSTAGE STAMP. WALKER HAS ALWAYS ADMIRED THE FAMOUS POET.

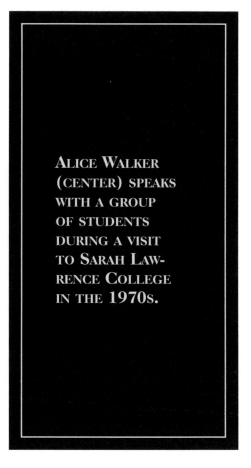

ALICE WALKER (CENTER) SPEAKS WITH A GROUP OF STUDENTS DURING A VISIT TO SARAH LAWRENCE COLLEGE IN THE 1970S.

For her second novel, *Meridian*, Walker drew on her own experiences. The book tells the story of a young woman and her struggles during the civil rights movement.

Critics praised *Meridian,* published in 1976. The successful book was coupled with personal troubles, however. That same year, she and Leventhal were divorced.

Walker decided she needed to start again, so she devoted herself to writing full-time. She resigned from *Ms.*, accepted a fellowship from the Guggenheim Foundation, and moved to San Francisco in 1979. There she became involved with Robert Allen, editor of *The Black Scholar*, and the two fell in love. Walker continued to write and finished *You Can't Keep a Good Woman Down*, another collection of short stories, which was published in 1981. It was the next year that would change everything.

ALICE WALKER AND ROBERT ALLEN, EDITOR OF *THE BLACK SCHOLAR*, BECAME INVOLVED IN THE 1980s. THEY LIVED IN CALIFORNIA.

Prizes and Politics

In 1982, Alice Walker published *The Color Purple*, a work that Peter S. Prescott in *Newsweek* magazine called "an American novel of permanent importance." The novel is about two black women, Shug and Celie, and the cruel men in their lives. The dialogue is realistic, and the book is a touching portrayal of human spirit and of women supporting one another. The book deals with Walker's "womanist" themes—ideas of black feminism and female strength.

As with her first novel, some critics complained that Walker's black male characters were portrayed too negatively. In spite of such criticism, *The Color Purple* was a best-seller and won the Pulitzer Prize and an American Book Award in 1983. Walker became the first African-American to win a Pulitzer Prize for fiction. Suddenly, she was famous.

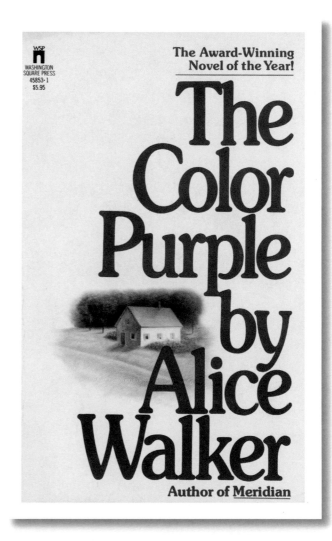

WSP
WASHINGTON
SQUARE PRESS
45853-1
$5.95

The Award-Winning
Novel of the Year!

The Color Purple by Alice Walker

Author of **Meridian**

THE BEST-SELLER *THE COLOR PURPLE* WAS PUBLISHED IN 1982.

That same year, she published *In Search of Our Mothers' Gardens*, a collection of essays, many of which explained her womanist ideas. Walker explains that a womanist is someone "committed to survival and wholeness of the entire people, male *and* female. A womanist . . . loves music. Loves dance. Loves the moon. *Loves* the spirit. Loves love and food and roundness. Loves struggle. . . . Loves herself. *Regardless.*"

Hollywood quickly took an interest in *The Color Purple*, and before long plans were made to turn the book into a movie. Steven Spielberg signed on as director and producer. Renowned musician Quincy Jones also joined the project as a producer.

During this period, Walker was suffering from **Lyme disease,** and there were days when she had very little energy. Nevertheless, she tried to take part in the production of the film. She did not write the screenplay, but she offered opinions about casting. Once filming began, she was often on the set.

Whoopi Goldberg, then a little-known comedian, was cast as Celie, and actor Danny Glover was given the role of Celie's husband. Actress Margaret Avery portrayed Shug. Oprah Winfrey, then a talk-show host known mostly in Chicago, had an important role as Sofia.

The end result was a dramatic film that received much attention after its 1985 release. Many of the actors' performances were powerful, and much of the music, written by Quincy Jones, was moving and effective. Walker was not entirely pleased with the story as it appeared on-screen, but she did praise many of the actors.

The movie went on to receive a number of Academy Award nominations. Some critics continued to criticize Walker's portrayal of black men. Yet she believed her writing was honest and realistic, and she tried not to let the criticism keep her from speaking her mind. To honor Walker, her sister Ruth started the Color Purple Foundation, a charity that raises money for education.

WHOOPI GOLDBERG, SHOWN HERE IN A STILL FROM *THE COLOR PURPLE*, WAS NOMINATED FOR AN ACADEMY AWARD FOR BEST ACTRESS FOR HER ROLE IN THAT 1985 FILM.

Walker did not let success go to her head. She continued to write and to speak out about issues that mattered to her. In 1984, she had published *Horses Make a Landscape Look More Beautiful*, her third collection of poems. Four years later, *Living by the Word* was published. Many critics praised that collection of essays and speeches as her most spiritual work so far.

In 1989, Walker published another novel, *The Temple of My Familiar*. Two years later, she published another volume of poetry, *Her Blue Body Everything We Know: Earthling Poems*.

In addition to writing novels and poetry for adults, Walker has also written books for children. The first was *To Hell with Dying*, based on the short story she wrote in college. It was published in 1988. Three years later, she published another one, *Finding the Green Stone*.

In 1988, Wild Trees Press, a publishing company that Walker and Allen had founded, had to be shut down. With this company, they had hoped to produce books that mattered to them. Such a business was a big risk, and in the end it lasted only four years.

Throughout her life, Walker has always taken on ideas and problems she sees as important. Among these is the treatment of girls in certain parts of Africa, which Walker criticized in her fifth novel, *Possessing the Secret of Joy*. She also journeyed to Africa with filmmaker Pratibha Parmar to make a **documentary** about this violent treatment. The film, released in 1993, and the book that Walker wrote to accompany it are both entitled *Warrior Marks*.

POET, NOVELIST, AND ESSAYIST ALICE WALKER SPEAKS TO HER READERS ACROSS GENDER AND RACE LINES.

In 1996, Walker published another collection of essays and journal entries. This work, titled *The Same River Twice: Honoring the Difficult,* explores the experience she had with Lyme disease, the problems in making *The Color Purple* film, the death of her mother, and the end of her relationship with Robert Allen.

The following year, Walker produced a collection of essays about her activism. *Anything We Love Can Be Saved: A Writer's Activism* reflects Walker's political work as well as her personal feelings. This collection tackles many causes including the environmental movement, the women's movement, and the antinuclear movement.

By the Light of My Father's Smile, Walker's sixth novel, was published in 1998. The story looks at the relationship between fathers and daughters, and it focuses on spiritual ideas such as guilt, forgiveness, and finding peace. Two years later, Walker published *The Way Forward Is with a Broken Heart,* a book loosely based on her experiences of living in the South with a white husband.

In reaction to the September 11, 2001, attacks on the United States, Walker published *Sent by Earth: A Message from the Grandmother Spirit after the Bombing of the World Trade Center and the Pentagon.* In this collection of poems and essays, she explores the violent times in which we live.

Walker's most recent book of poetry, published in 2003, is titled *Absolute Trust in the Goodness of the Earth.* In this collection, her poems focus on romance, home cooking, and racial diversity, among other things. They also express her love and gratitude for our planet.

ALICE WALKER, SHOWN HERE IN **2002**, CONTINUES TO WRITE AND SPEAK OUT ABOUT TODAY'S ISSUES.

Today, Alice Walker continues to travel and take an interest in many political causes. She doesn't hesitate to voice her opinions to members of Congress, presidents, and other world leaders—and even to disagree with them. She is quick to speak out against racism and sexism, and she supports keeping historical and natural areas the way they are.

A **vegetarian** and an enthusiastic gardener, Walker is still exploring spiritual matters and personal limits. She pours her thoughts into her writing to enrich the lives of her audiences. She reminds her readers that "We are indeed the world. Only if we have reason to fear what is in our hearts need we fear for the planet. Teach yourself peace. Pass it on."

ALICE WALKER AND HER DAUGHTER, REBECCA, PARTICIPATE IN A VOTER RALLY. LIKE HER MOTHER, REBECCA WALKER IS AN AUTHOR AND ACTIVIST.

Timeline

1944	Alice Malsenior Walker is born on February 9 in Eatonton, Georgia.
1952	Walker is blinded in one eye after being shot in the eye with a BB gun.
1961	Walker enrolls at Spelman College in Atlanta, Georga.
1963	Walker accepts a scholarship and transfers to Sarah Lawrence College in Bronxville, New York.
1965	Walker graduates from Sarah Lawrence and then works in Georgia for the civil rights movement.
1966	Walker continues her civil rights work in Mississippi.
1967	Alice Walker and Mel Leventhal are married on March 17 and then move to Mississippi.
1969	Walker gives birth to her daughter, Rebecca Grant.
1970	*The Third Life of Grange Copeland*, Walker's first novel, is published.
1972	Walker accepts a teaching position at Wellesley College.
1973	Walker honors poet Zora Neale Hurston by placing a headstone at her grave.
1974	Walker moves back to New York with Leventhal.
1976	Walker and Leventhal are divorced. *Meridian* is published.
1979	Walker moves to San Francisco and becomes involved with Robert Allen.
1982	*The Color Purple* is published.
1983	Walker receives the Pulitzer Prize for fiction and an American Book Award for *The Color Purple*.
1984	Walker and Allen found Wild Trees Press.
1985	*The Color Purple* film is released.
1988	*Living by the Word* and *To Hell with Dying* are published. Wild Trees Press goes out of business.
1991	*Finding the Green Stone* is published.
1993	The documentary *Warrior Marks* is released.
1996	*The Same River Twice: Honoring the Difficult* is published.
1997	*Anything We Love Can Be Saved: A Writer's Activism* is published.
1998	*By the Light of My Father's Smile* is published.
2000	*The Way Forward Is with a Broken Heart* is published.
2001	Following the September 11 attacks, Walker publishes *Sent by Earth: A Message from the Grandmother Spirit after the Bombing of the World Trade Center and the Pentagon*.
2003	*Absolute Trust in the Goodness of the Earth* is published.

Glossary

activist (AK-tih-vist)
An activist is someone who takes direct action for a particular cause. Walker is an activist for many issues.

civil rights (SIV-il RITES)
Civil rights are rights that all citizens should have, no matter what their race or background is. Walker worked for the civil rights movement in the 1960s.

depression (di-PRESH-un)
Depression is a feeling of great sadness. Walker suffered from depression in college.

documentary (dok-yuh-MEN-tuh-ree)
A documentary is a film about real events and people. Walker worked on a documentary called *Warrior Marks*.

fellowship (FEL-oh-ship)
A fellowship is an award of money given by a college or other organization. Fellowships often helped Walker live as a writer.

feminist (FEM-uh-nist)
A feminist is a person who believes that women should have the same political, economic, and social rights as men. Walker calls herself a "womanist," which is her word for a black feminist.

Harlem Renaissance (HAR-lum REN-uh-sahnss)
The Harlem Renaissance was a time in the 1920s marked by great artistic activity among African-Americans. Zora Neale Hurston was a writer during the Harlem Renaissance.

Lyme disease (LIME duh-ZEEZ)
Lyme disease is an illness spread by the bite of a tick. People suffering from the disease often have chills and a fever. Walker got Lyme disease in the 1980s.

Pulitzer Prize (PUH-lit-sur PRIZE)
Pulitzer Prizes are great honors awarded each year for excellence in literature and journalism. Walker was the first African-American to win a Pulitzer Prize for fiction.

sexism (SEK-sism)
Sexism is the practice of mistreating a person based on his or her sex. Walker believes that sexism can take many forms.

sharecroppers (SHAIR-krop-urs)
Sharecroppers are people who farm land that belongs to someone else. Walker's parents were sharecroppers and earned very little money.

spirituality (spihr-uh-choo-WAL-uh-tee)
Spirituality is a sense of religious faith and values. Themes of spirituality are present in much of Walker's work.

vegetarian (vej-uh-TER-ee-uhn)
A vegetarian is someone who eats food made only from plants and sometimes dairy products and eggs. Walker's beliefs about the natural world led her to become a vegetarian.

welfare (WEL-fair)
Welfare is money and other help given by the government to people in need. Walker worked in a welfare department when she was a young woman.

Index

Further Information

Books

Gentry, Tony. *Alice Walker.* Broomall, Penn.: Chelsea House, 1993.

Lazo, Caroline Evensen. *Alice Walker: Freedom Writer*. Minneapolis: Lerner, 2000.

Rediger, Pat. *Great African Americans in Literature.* New York: Crabtree Publishing Company, 1996.

Walker, Alice. *Langston Hughes: American Poet*. New York: HarperCollins Children's Books, 2002.

Web Sites

Visit our homepage for lots of links about Alice Walker:

http://www.childsworld.com/links.html

Note to Parents, Teachers, and Librarians:
We routinely verify our Web links to make sure they're safe,
active sites—so encourage your readers to check them out!

About the Author

Lucia Raatma received her bachelor's degree in English literature from the University of South Carolina and her master's degree in cinema studies from New York University. She has written a wide range of books for young people. When she is not researching or writing, she enjoys going to movies, practicing yoga, and spending time with her husband, daughter, and golden retriever. She lives in New York.